A GUITAR, A BIBLE, & A SHOTGUN

Linda Hudson Hoagland

Linda Hudson Hoagland

copyright © 2018 Linda Hudson Hoagland
ISBN 13: 978-1727237948
ISBN 10: 1727237943

A GUITAR, A BIBLE, AND A SHOTGUN

ACKNOWLEDGEMENTS

I would like to thank the late Tommy Jones for having the trust and faith that I would write this book as he wanted it written.

Publish America of Baltimore for originally publishing this book as *Living Life for Other* in 2011.

Victoria Fletcher, a fellow author and publisher, for preparing this book for printing.

DEDICATION

I, Tommy Jones, want to dedicate this book to my Grandmother Arena Pritt Jones, to my dog George, and to all of my pets that came after him throughout my life. My pets were my only true friends. I loved them all and I know they all loved me. That is why we do all we can do for pets. We have a small mission to give food out to people with pets. We would like to start a foundation for pets someday.

A GUITAR, A BIBLE, AND A SHOTGUN

INTRODUCTION

My name is Linda Hudson Hoagland and I am a writer from Tazewell, Virginia. My genres have been mysteries, fiction, and nonfiction.

It has been hard trying to become recognized as a writer, an author, of what I hope are good books. But, like all forms of writing, books are at the mercy of the subjective reader.

I finally wrangled an appearance on the local television program called "In Focus" that is filmed in the WVVA studios in Bluefield, West Virginia.

My appearance on "In Focus" was a new and exciting moment in my life. I had no idea that my appearance would prompt a telephone call from Tommy and Sharon Jones to the television station requesting information on how they could get in touch with me.

The young lady that conducted the interview called me and asked if it was okay to give my telephone number to the Joneses.

"Of course," I replied, as I smiled from ear to ear.

Tommy and Sharon called me and asked for help in writing a book about Tommy.

It is Tommy's life, so I tried to make it solely Tommy's book.

No money has passed between us except for postage that Tommy seems compelled to pay.

We've never actually met face-to-face, but I'm proud to say that Tommy and Sharon Jones are my friends.

Linda Hudson Hoagland
Author

A GUITAR, A BIBLE, AND A SHOTGUN

CHAPTER 1
CHILDREN CAN BE CRUEL

Young Tommy Jones was not going to find the prospects of a happy and prosperous life in the bleak, hardscrabble coal camp in rural West Virginia.

Families eked out a hand-to-mouth existence in the post-World War II days. For Jones, it seemed as if fate had dealt him a worse hand than his contemporaries.

The fact that Jones had no legal father of record was soon discovered by one of his peers. The cruelty of children surpassed the normal restraints of an adult who was more apt to exercise control. Jones was the object of taunts, not only because of his lack of legitimacy; but racially, when word spread through the little community of Vaughn that his suspected father was of Sicilian descent.

It went almost without saying; Jones was bombarded with ugly, derogatory names when the "B" word grew old with them. They used such ethnic slurs as "wop", "nigger", and "grease ball", which made it easy to understand why Jones had little desire to share his boyhood in the tiny schoolhouse with the other mostly cruel children.

With the assistance of a midwife, fetched by his grandfather, Floyd Bratton Jones, in a mile and one-half trek walking down a railroad track, Jones was born at home December 28, 1940.

"I lived in a really old coal company house that was probably built in the 1880's. It was a one-story house, but I can't remember the name of the coal company that owned it," he said. "There was a store and a church facing the railroad. That's how they got everything into the community."

Jones' sister, Brenda, was also born out of wedlock, and both children were put in the care of Bratton and his wife, Arena.

"My mom later got married, but I don't remember just when," he said. "My mom was like a party girl and she admitted it. She just didn't want the responsibility of raising us. Later she got married and I have a half brother that is eight years younger."

The mother remained at the grandparents' home until she married.

In a manner of speaking, Bratton was a jack of all trades although he devoted his work years largely to mining coal – the bedrock industry of West Virginia decades ago.

A GUITAR, A BIBLE, AND A SHOTGUN

"He had worked on the railroad when he was younger, and even had one of his eyes put out while working there," Jones said.

Bratton was assigned to a particular section where the crew was driving spokes and a piece of wayward metal flew up from a spike directly into his left eye.

"It was a bad thing for him because it happened when he was young," Jones said.

Bratton was about fifty when he took in the two grandchildren, a fact Jones verified when he discovered his grandfather's mining certificate. There had been a considerable delay in Bratton obtaining the required paperwork after going into the mining industry.

"Grandpa," he asked, "why did you wait so long to get the papers?"

"Well," Bratton explained, "back in those days, people didn't need them."

CHAPTER 2
CHILDHOOD TURMOIL

Turmoil thrust itself into the boyhood of Tommy Jones, but he can look back with some joy at the memory of a teacher named Mrs. Broughman who understood his circumstances and tried her best to encourage him to stay in school and develop what talent he possessed.

The task of keeping Jones interested was not easy. More often than not, Jones fell under the spell of the easy way out by simply heading into the woods, dogs in tow, to play hooky. That was an act that made him more than familiar with the local truant officer.

A drunken, abusive uncle, and later on, a step-father who displayed the same negative traits, complicated matters for the Jones children.

"We didn't live with him," Jones recalled. "You know how that is in some families."

Sharon, who is Jones' second wife, understands that bad feeling. She went through the same thing in her life except her bad experience was with her real father.

"He was an alcoholic. He also made and sold moonshine when we were young. I was twelve years old when he left home and thirteen when I found out that my mom and dad were never married," explains Sharon. "There were three girls and one boy. I was the youngest."

Jones talks kindly of his first wife by calling her a good woman but simply says the two of them couldn't get along. Their differences couldn't be reconciled; so, they decided to call off the marriage.

"She wanted other things in life and I couldn't afford them," he said. "I think that was the way it was. At first, we got along pretty good. I wasn't a party guy. I never did do anything bad, but we got divorced."

Even today, Jones appears to feel the ill-effects of childhood teasing over his ethnicity.

"They called me all kinds of names," he said.

Jones learned of his suspected Sicilian heritage from his grandmother while the dysfunctional family lived around Campbell's Creek outside Charleston. A child cannot understand the contempt that was carried in such slurs, and Jones certainly was no exception when it came to the constant taunting he endured. All that he knew was that it cut deeply into his soul.

It seemed the family was always on the move and he didn't start school until the age of nine, about three years late for the average student.

"All I got was a fifth-grade education," he said. "I just quit because I was so far behind, but I learned how to read and write pretty good. Grandpa taught me, but it was Mrs. Broughman who really put me on the track."

CHAPTER 3
COATS

When we moved to Greenbrier County, Brenda was starting into the second grade. Grandmother and grandfather would buy us as many clothes as they could and sometimes our mom would help us get some clothes whenever she could spare the money. We were told no one could afford to get Brenda a coat.

We lived in Quinwood, a coal company town on a mountain. It was a busy little town in those days. We even had a doctor's office. The two doctors that ran the office were Dr. Leach and Dr. Todd. They pooled their resources and bought Brenda a coat. She loved that coat. She was so proud of it.

The gift of a much-needed coat planted something in my mind. We would buy coats at flea markets or yard sales and give them to people who needed them when we were giving out food for the mission.

We went to the flea markets and yard sales all summer long and bought coats. We gave them away at our food bank. Every fall, we would ship them out to a lot of different places in the USA. We have done this for years now; even during the years before the food bank. There is a need and someone should do something about that need, was my way of thinking.

After I got sick, we haven't been able to do much with coat shipping. Sharon said that I have a coat fetish that I can't pass up nice coat without buying it. She always looks for me to come home with anywhere from one to ten (or more) coats.

Brenda's new coat is why I still like to help people with coats to this day.

CHAPTER 4
GEORGE TO THE RESCUE

One of Tommy's more emotional times involved a husky, a cur dog named George. Jones was so moved by the telling of this time in his life that he broke down and had to get his wife to finish the account.

Jones' grandmother used the shaggy mutt as a babysitter of sorts, telling him to lie down beside little Tommy and keep him safe while she went outside to hang up freshly washed clothes or to fetch firewood to cook meals and to heat the old dwelling.

Jones and George, in a real sense, grew up together and were practically inseparable.

Resembling a collie with long white and black hair intermingled, George proved to be more than a constant companion.

One wintry day, Jones was stepping gingerly across a hewn-out log used as a makeshift bridge across a swirling creek when he lost his balance and tumbled into the chilly water. Unable to right himself, Jones kept tumbling over and over in the rolling stream while making some futile efforts to grab hold of something, anything that would put a halt to his momentum.

Nothing helped the frantic youngster. His hands would slide off the slippery, protruding rocks. The brush and tree branches sticking out from the creek bank were too far away to be of any help. He tried to scream but the sound was cut short when his mouth filled with water.

George raced across the log bridge to where the grandfather was standing, and jumped in the rapidly flowing water, allowing Tommy to grab his long fur and ride him out of the creek. It was life imitating art, a real-life episode that reminded Jones of an Elvis Presley tune entitled "Old Shep."

A few years later, George would be called upon for a repeat performance to rescue Jones' sister, Brenda.

"Tommy can hardly talk about George," said Sharon, his wife of many years, "and with good reason."

A mean-spirited person, whom Jones suspected was a neighbor down the road from him, poisoned George. As Jones turned up spades of dirt for his pet's grave, the woman leered at him; so, the youngster scooped up a handful of dirt and flung it at her.

"He was pretty sure it was her because she and her family didn't like animals," Mrs. Jones relates. "Her excuse for doing it was that Tommy was a bastard. Come to find out, she had two of her own. We didn't find that out until a short while ago."

Jones even thought about heaving the shovel at the woman, given the depth of feeling he had for George, and the heart pain he was feeling over his pet's death.

"Tommy was glad that his grandmother stopped him," she said. "He's real soft-hearted when it comes to animals."

Linda Hudson Hoagland

CHAPTER 5
GRANDMOTHER'S STORIES

These are some of the stories our grandmother used to tell us when we were sitting around the fireplace.

There was always a feud or two going on through the families.

Grandmother told us a story about her sister Josephine; we called her Aunt Josie.

Aunt Josie was married to a man called Dewey Graham. People were afraid of him. He was sort of a bully and just plain mean.

The mines where he worked were on strike so a few of the men would get together and play poker.

We had a distant cousin who everyone called "Penny" Pritt.

Well, one night Penny and three other men got together and decided to kill Dewey.

There was a poker game at Dewey's house where they all sat down to play. After a few hands, the man in front of Dewey jumped under the table and grabbed Dewey's feet. The men on both sides of him grabbed his arms and pulled them behind his chair. Penny grabbed a knife and cut Dewey's throat and killed him.

A GUITAR, A BIBLE, AND A SHOTGUN

No one knows what happened after that killing and no one knows Penny's real name or what happened to him.

Grandmother said it happened in Kanawha County in the early 1920's.

Another story grandmother told us was about her daughter, Anne Stone. She married Roy H. Price and they lived in Alum Junction in Kanawha County, West Virginia, where they had eight children.

Roy was a security guard for the C & O Railroad when he contracted tuberculosis and was hospitalized for a long period of time. One day, he just walked out of the hospital. He was dressed only in his pajamas. He knew the railroad tracks so well he decided to walk home.

When he walked through the front door of his home, he and Ann began arguing. After spewing several loud, angry words, he walked into the bedroom, got his .38 caliber out of the closet, loaded it, and walked back into the kitchen.

Anne turned and started to walk out into another room. Before she cleared the threshold, he called her name. When she turned around, he shot her once in the chest. As she fell, he shot her once in the back. He stepped over her and walked outside into the back yard where he shot himself in the right temple.

Linda Hudson Hoagland

Some kin people called my grandmother's neighbor. They came to the house and told grandmother what had happened. My grandmother asked someone to take her to be with her daughter.

This happened September 4, 1940. Anne was thirty-seven years old and Roy was thirty-four.

When my sister, Brenda, and I were small we asked grandmother if we could build an upstairs at the old coal company house where we lived in Vaughan. Brenda, George, and I found some boards to use to construct our upstairs.

Grandmother told us we could if we didn't tear up anything and to be careful not to fall through the ceiling.

We were so happy because we always wanted an upstairs like a rich cousin of ours had. His name was Tildon Hanshaw and he lived in Vaughan, too.

Brenda, George, and I started to carry the boards up the ladder that we had found hidden in the closet. Every trip we made, George went, too. We started to lay down the boards to get them lined up so we could nail them into place. It was really dusty and we got really dirty.

Grandmother was sweeping the living room and, all of a sudden, Brenda fell though the living room ceiling right in front of grandmother. Brenda wasn't hurt but she started crying because she knew that we were going to get a whipping.

A few minutes after Brenda fell, George fell through the same hole.

Dust and coal dirt were swirling everywhere.

I stuck my head through the hole and grandmother was looking at me, standing there with her hands on her hips.

She told me, "Get on down here and get your whipping, too."

After we got our punishments, granny handed us a bar of soap and told us, "Go down to the creek and take a bath and give George one, too."

So, needless to say, that was the end of our upstairs building and grandpa had to fix the ceiling.

Brenda, George, and I decided to build a pirate ship. Actually, it was a small raft. We put a stove pipe on it and called it a cannon. We were so proud of it. We would go down to the creek and get on our pirate ship. Brenda was on one side, me on the other, and George was in the middle. The creek was low and about twenty feet wide. We would play pirates floating from one side to the other.

One night we got a real heavy and hard rain. The next morning, we went to check on our ship. It was gone.

Brenda and I started crying.

"What's wrong?" asked Granny.

"Our pirate ship is gone," we both cried.

To settle us down, Granny told us, "Probably another pirate ship came by during the night and stole it."

It did settle us down, but it didn't help George. Every day, we would see George sitting on the creek bank just looking up and down the creek. We think he missed our pirate ship as much as we did. He just kept waiting for the ship to come back.

CHAPTER 6
UNCLE HENRY PRITT

Another story our Grandmother Arena used to tell us was about her brother, Henry Pritt, who was my great uncle. This happened in the early twenties.

Henry was of average height. There was a big bully that used to harass and bully everyone that was smaller than he was. This went on every day.

Finally, Uncle Henry got fed up with him and told him, "Come on down behind my big pile of lumber and we will settle this once and for all."

The only one that came out from behind that lumber pile was Uncle Henry.

Uncle Henry had shot and killed the big bully.

It was ruled as self-defense by the legal authorities.

There was no more bullying after that.

No one, especially the Pritts, would talk about it except my Grandmother Arena.

Grandmother had a son that she named after her brother, Henry. My mom, Alice, named my half-brother Henry after her brother. Bill went to the court house to register baby Henry's name. On his way there he got drunk and turned his name in backwards. Instead of Henry William Clark, he turned it in as William Henry Clark, but we called him Buddy. When Henry, "Buddy," was in his twenties, he ordered a copy of his birth certificate and found out his name was backwards. Before discovering the mistake, he and his wife had a son and they named him Henry William Clark, Jr. after his father, or so they thought.

CHAPTER 7
LITTLE BEAR

A cousin of ours had a little black dog named Little Bear. Every time they went out of town, they would bring Little Bear over to stay with us.

George, my dog, and Little Bear were real good buddies.

Our cousin lived two hollows and two small hills over from us.

Little Bear was a small, long-haired, fuzzy dog. He looked a lot like a little black bear.

We also had a cousin that we all called Uncle Muck. I don't know why we called him Uncle Muck but everyone did. He was a preacher.

At that time, grandmother, grandfather, Brenda, and I had a lot of chickens. We gave eggs to all of our neighbors including Uncle Muck. He wore a pair of suspender overalls and usually one side was loose and hanging down. Sometimes he wore a tee shirt and sometimes he didn't.

One night, George and Little Bear started growling and barking. They went running off of the porch to the chicken house. Grandmother grabbed a shot gun and we ran out the back door carrying a flashlight to the chicken house.

George and Little Bear brought someone out of the chicken house. George had one pants leg in his mouth and Little Bear had the other tugging on it. The man filling those pants fell to the ground.

Grandmother shined the light on him and said, "Why, it's Uncle Muck. What are you doing in our chicken house?"

"Stealing eggs," said Uncle Muck.

"Get up from there," said grandmother.

"I will after you call George and Little Bear off of me," he said.

Grandmother called George and Little Bear. They ran to her and sat down on each side of her.

Uncle Muck started crying and told grandmother that he wanted to get saved again so he and grandmother prayed together.

The next day he came to our house and told us that they were having a tent revival down next to Charleston and he wanted all of us to come down the first night, tomorrow night.

"Sure, we'll come and probably bring some of the neighbors with us," answered grandmother.

A GUITAR, A BIBLE, AND A SHOTGUN

She asked her son and his wife (Uncle Bud and Aunt Lil) to take us down there. We all loaded up in Uncle Bud's 1934 Chrysler four-door. We even took George and Little Bear with us. Grandmother invited a couple of neighbors to go with us because it was only a couple of miles away from our home.

When we got down there, they were all singing and shouting.

Everyone got out of the car (except me and the dogs) and they went into the tent. They sat on the back row of seats.

What we didn't know was that they had snakes. It was a snake-handling church.

Little Bear and George started barking and jumping from the back seat to the front seat over and over again.

I leaned over the steering wheel to see what they kept barking at. When I did, I knocked the car out of gear and the car rolled down a little knoll. We rolled right into the middle of the tent.

There we sat looking at Uncle Muck.

The congregation all started dancing and talking a funny language.

Then there was a snake thrown across the hood of the car.

I jumped into the back seat and George and Little Bear kept growling and chewing the dashboard of the car trying to get to the snake. They hated snakes.

Uncle Bud got into the car and started it. He backed it up onto the little knoll.

When we looked up, everyone was running back to the car. They were all real white-faced and nervous when they jumped into the car.

All the way home, everything that moved was thought to be a snake.

George and Little Bear kept growling and barking as they looked out the back window. I was sure they wanted to go back and kill the snakes.

CHAPTER 8
A LITTLE ABOUT UNCLE MUCK

I want to tell you a little about Uncle Muck. His mother was a Jones, but no one can remember her first name. Everyone said that she was a real pretty woman and she was a distant cousin. She met a man from New Orleans, Louisiana. He was a Cajun. His last name was Boudreaux. He was Uncle Muck's father.

Uncle Muck went by the name of Reverend Uncle Muck Boudreaux. I don't know why everyone called him Uncle Muck. He was a lot like me. He was born out of wedlock. In other words, we were both bastards.

We lived down around Hughes Creek in 1947 or 1948. Our Uncle Bud had a pretty big car at the time so we all decided to go to the company store. In the car was grandmother, Uncle Bud, Aunt Lil, George, Little Bear, and me. We loved going to the company store, especially on the weekend because we got ice cream on the weekends.

Grandmother decided to stop and get another friend and family member. Her name was Liza Jane Jones and she was also a cousin. She was a real good singer and would sing all of the way there and all of the way home. She could sing country, rhythm and blues, bluegrass, blues, and religious songs. On the way over, we stopped and asked Uncle Muck if he wanted to go with us. He said he had a lot to do. So, we all left and someone in the car said that he probably had to go check his still before he wrote out his next day sermon.

The company store was burning down. The people who owned the store stood there watching it burn. They told everyone that if they saw anything, they could use to just take it. There were a lot of things laying on the ground, so we picked up a few things. Uncle Bud picked up a stool and put it into the trunk of the car. We had quite a few things in the trunk, so we had to leave the trunk lid open.

On the way home, everyone that passed us would wave and holler at us. We never could hear what they were saying because we could hear a siren blaring. George and Little Bear hated sirens. Every time they heard one, they would bark and howl.

A law car (constable) came up beside Uncle Bud's car and hollered really loud to Uncle Bud asking him if he could hear. Uncle Bud told him no, not too well, so he motioned for Uncle Bud to pull over.

A GUITAR, A BIBLE, AND A SHOTGUN

George and Little Bear finally stopped barking when he pulled over and the law car cut his siren off. The mountain people called all of the constable cars "law cars" because they were unmarked.

When Uncle Bud pulled over, we could see smoke swirling every where. We all got out of the car and the law told Uncle Bud that his trunk was on fire. The stool Uncle Bud had taken had started burning again. We had to take everything out of the trunk and put the fire out. We all got back into the car. We let Liza Jane out at her house and we went on home.

Grandfather asked, "Where did you all get all this stuff?"

We told him that the company store burned down and that the owners had given us all of these things. Grandfather couldn't believe that they would give anyone anything.

We don't know what happened to Reverend Uncle Muck and his mother after we moved to Quinwood. We heard that his mother and him moved to New Orleans and were living with Reverend Uncle Muck's father. I sure do miss him. I wish I could see him and his mother again.

CHAPTER 9
COUSINS

I have quite a few cousins down next to Charleston and in a lot of the other counties. One cousin I had was telling me that quite a few years ago, one of our other cousins had stopped at a bar down in Charleston to talk to a friend of his.

What he didn't know was that the law had an undercover sting going on in the bar. A few automobile dealerships were switching vehicle identification numbers (VIN) on several vehicles. The law had followed some of the suspects into the bar.

I have all kinds of kin people in and around all the counties around Charleston using the names of Jones, Pritt, Stone, Barnett, Price, Foster and Gearadonos among others.

My cousin was talking to his friend in the bar that night. He had no idea that there was a sting going on in the bar. There were FBI and all kinds of cops in there. He had just stopped to talk to a friend and to have a beer with him. The bar was crowded and all of a sudden, a brawl broke out in the bar.

Well, my cousin picked up a beer bottle and hit a man over the head with it.

A GUITAR, A BIBLE, AND A SHOTGUN

They tore the bar up with so many fighting. The bar owner called the town police. They came and took everyone to jail. They charged everyone with something,

My cousin really didn't know what was going on. After a couple of days, they finally figured out that my cousin did not have anything to do with any of the things that they were investigating. That was when my cousin found out that the man he hit over the head with a beer bottle was an FBI agent.

I think they never did find out about who was changing the VIN number on the vehicles at that time.

Later, I heard they eventually found out that it was the used car salesman that was changing the VIN numbers at two or three used car lots.

CHAPTER 10
BERRY PICKING

When I was young, grandmother and I used to go down the road to Uncle Andy's house at Campbell's Creek in the summer to help his wife with canning and cleaning. Her name was Marge.

One day they decided to go berry picking. There was her mother and some friends of theirs, about seven of them in all. Marge's son Jerry was seven years old and they took him along to beat the ground with a stick to scare the snakes away from the berry patch. They wanted me to go along with them, but grandmother told them that she wanted me to stay there and help her.

I was so mad at her.

"Why wouldn't you let me go," I asked grandmother after they all left.

"Wait a little while and you will know why," she answered.

Well, about thirty minutes later, we heard loud hollering and loud talking and berry buckets were thrown at the porch.

Grandmother and I went to the door and grandmother asked, "What happened? What's wrong?"

Marge told her that Jerry had forgotten his cigarettes at home.

A GUITAR, A BIBLE, AND A SHOTGUN

My grandmother had seen Jerry's cigarettes on the end table.

They were all so mad because he had forgotten his cigarettes, so he had to come back and no berry picking got done. As I said previously, he was only seven years old at the time.

His mother always gave him hot toddies, an alcohol mixture, three or four times a day. He died at the age of fifty with a massive heart attack.

CHAPTER 11
A REAL MEAN DRUNK

My mother's husband came from Virginia. He had a real bad temper. He wasn't a really big man, about five feet nine inches tall. He didn't like Brenda or me at all because we were Alice's bastard children.

That's why we always lived with our Grandmother Arena and Grandfather Bratton Jones.

Bill Clark was my mother's husband. He was a real mean drunk and he drank a lot.

We lived about thirty miles east of Charleston up Hughes Creek. We lived beside the Kanawha River in a small mining town. Grandfather was a night watchman or guard for the coal company.

Bill and his two brothers, George and Shorty Clark, worked inside the mine. Bill and mom were staying with us at the time.

One day, Bill and some of his drinking buddies decided to walk up the road and play poker under a big tree up from our house.

One of the men's name was Horny Hornsby. He used to like our mom.

Bill found out about it. He called Horny out into the road. He pulled a knife and cut Horny's stomach open from one side to the other.

Someone came up to our house and told us that Bill had cut Horny's guts out and they were jumping up and down in the middle of the road.

Someone called the sheriff, constable, and an ambulance. By the time the law and ambulance got there, Bill was gone.

We don't know how he left. He couldn't keep cars because every time he would get drunk, he would wreck them. He never had any operator's license, so we just figured that he just took off walking.

They thought Horny was going to die but he got better in about a month.

After Bill found out there were no charges brought against him, he came back from Virginia where he was staying at his home place. He picked up mom and Buddy and they moved to Greenbrier County.

Our mom didn't care for Brenda and me very much but when Bill got a job at a coal company at Quinwood, mom would send grandmother money to help with us sometimes.

CHAPTER 12
MOM'S HUSBAND

They found out that Bill Clark, mom's husband, had a bad heart in the early 60's. They told him that he had only a short time to live. The last two months of his life, he did quit drinking. Even after they told him about his heart, he still got drunk a few more times.

One winter day, after a lot of snow fell in Quinwood; Bill Clark got drunk and was staggering home from the beer joint. Mom, Bill, and Buddy lived down on the main road. Grandmother, grandfather, Brenda, and I lived a few houses up from them in a trailer camp. That's why everyone called us "white trash from the trailer camp." Our house was about a hundred yards from the end.

Bill would leave his house and walk to the beer joint and get drunk a lot.

He was staggering home and fell into the driveway below their house. His feet were sticking out into the road. The Mayor of Quinwood drove by and saw Bill lying in the driveway.

The mayor thought that Bill had had a heart attack. He stopped to help Bill. When he reached down to help Bill to his feet, Bill hit him right in the stomach. I didn't know anything about it until a couple of days later.

I stopped to buy gas and the mayor was there at the filling station. He told me what Bill had done. There was a crowd of people standing around when he told me.

I told him I couldn't help what Bill did. I got into my car and left.

It wasn't very long, a few months after that, that Bill had a heart attack and died at home.

CHAPTER 13
THE JONES BROTHERS

This story happened when grandfather and his brothers were all in their twenties. There was Grandfather Bratton and four brothers: Joe, Jeff, Lee, and John Jones. They all decided to go walking down the road one evening. As they were going out the door, Uncle Joe reached up to the wall beside the door and got the .38 caliber revolver off the wall. He stuck it down his belt and pants.

"We might need this," was all he said.

There was a family of about seven people that lived down the road from them. They owned a lot of land all around them.

Back then, there were no bridges across the creeks. You either walked or rode through the creeks. The road was a county road, but they still didn't want anyone going up or down the road.

Those were some mean boys and they decided to stop the Jones brothers as they were walking through the creek.

"That's our creek and we don't want you Jones boys crossing our creek any more."

They started a fight with the Jones boys.

A GUITAR, A BIBLE, AND A SHOTGUN

There was one fellow that had Uncle Joe on his hands and knees, beating on his back. That's when Uncle Joe pulled the .38 caliber out of his pants and shot over his shoulder two times. The one beating Uncle Joe started screaming and those so-called mean boys all ran off.

When the Jones boys got up, they were all running.

Uncle Joe had shot the one in the private parts that had him pinned down.

No charges were ever brought against Uncle Joe. One good thing did come out of it and that was that every time anyone would go down the road, they would tip their hats to the so-called mean boys, even the Jones' family.

They never did have any more trouble.

CHAPTER 14
MOUNTAIN MUSIC

The Jones boys were real easy going, hardworking, and they all had moonshine stills up in the mountains. Every so often, they would come down from the mountains and play some good old mountain music.

Grandfather could play a harmonica. Grandfather had some friends that would play music with them. They were Tom Taylor, who played a guitar; his brother, John, played a fiddle, and Howard Smith played a mandolin. They would play for hours. They were really good musicians.

Sometimes they would all go up to the stills and play music, too. Back in those days they never called it moonshine. In the summer, they called it snake bite medicine. In the winter, it was called cough medicine. It took me a long time to figure out what they were talking about.

This music happened up one of the hollows in Kanawha County. I wish we had a tape of some of that old mountain music. Those men could really play.

I'm sorry to say there is very little of that kind of music around these days.

A GUITAR, A BIBLE, AND A SHOTGUN

CHAPTER 15
ROGER COTRELL

One of my cousins down around Charleston was Roger Cottrell. I knew him and liked him really well. He told everyone that I was his favorite cousin.

He was a lot younger than me and he was a big guy. He was always jumping rope and he was really good with a punching bag.

Everyone always told him that he should have become a boxer, but he never did. He was big and tough.

Most people that didn't know him were scared of him. He was tough, but he was a really nice guy.

He was all the time getting into trouble when he was younger. The law was all the time taking him to Anthony Correctional Center in Greenbrier County. Then he would always stop off to see me when his kin people would go to get him out of jail.

He was arrested quite a few times in Charleston. On two different occasions the police beat him up really bad. So, after the second time, he sued them and after the judge saw the video tapes, he won both cases. Another cousin told me that he would go on big spending sprees and buy cars, motorcycles, and whatever he wanted but he would always put everything into someone else's name. He lived with his girlfriend.

He knew that I liked old cars and when he was younger, he decided to bring me an old car. Only there was a catch in his plan-- it was stolen. He stole it down next to Charleston somewhere and he started to Rainelle with it. He came to a place called Chimney Corner. It's a real sharp u-turn and right below the u-turn you go left to get to Rainelle. The right takes you back in the direction of Fayetteville and Beckley.

Well, luck was on my side and not so much on his that evening because he turned right. The law stopped him in Beckley. The people that owned the car were so glad to get their car back they wouldn't press charges against him. Luck was on his side then.

After that, he called me and told me what he had done. I didn't even know what to say. Till this day I still laugh about it and I really am glad he took the wrong road that day.

After he won his lawsuit against the Charleston Police, someone told him that his girlfriend was seeing a police officer. One evening, he followed her and saw her with that police officer. He turned around, went back home, and waited for her to arrive.

A GUITAR, A BIBLE, AND A SHOTGUN

When she came home, they got into a really big argument that lasted for quite a while. Then – she pulled out a gun and shot him in the chest (heart), killing him instantly. At least, that's what we heard.

We had an uncle that lived not far from us at Hughes Creek. One day, grandmother, Brenda, George, and I decided to visit him for a while. My Uncle "Bud" got drunk a lot back then and every time he got drunk, he always wanted to die by a train running over him and the railroad tracks were not far from his house. Aunt Lil, grandmother, Brenda, George, and I went out to the railroad tracks. Sure enough, there laid Uncle Bud across the railroad tracks.

"You shouldn't be carrying on this way," Granny told him.

"Why do you want to kill yourself?" Aunt Lil asked him.

"I want to die and I want the train to come and hit me and kill me," he would say.

"Bud, get up from there. You are not going to die today or any other day on that railroad track," Granny told him.

"What do you mean by that?" asked Uncle Bud.

"Bud, that train hasn't run up here for five years now."

Our Aunt Lil was a real nice woman. She loved Brenda and me and we loved her. She was all the time buying us things. Sometimes she would take change and bury it out next to her flowers.

"You go out next to the fence, next to my flower bed. If you find any money, I will walk with you down to the store to buy a pop or candy," Aunt Lil would say.

We would always find money.

The first time Brenda and I ever saw a Santa Claus was when Aunt Lil took us down to Charleston. That was such a big thrill for Brenda and me.

CHAPTER 16
INSPIRATION FROM
UNION MISSION

It was in his childhood that the seeds of his future calling in adult life would take root. Jones was deeply impressed by the generosity displayed to his family by "Brother" Pat Withrow, as the family came to call him, while he worked for the Union Mission in Charleston.

"He gave us food," Jones said. "We didn't eat there continuously, but he gave everybody food when they didn't have it." He was a really great guy. He always made us feel important just by talking to us.

"When we were hungry or needed clothes, I could see where they were giving us stuff. In the back of my mind, I always wanted to do something like that."

My grandmother told me once, "If you ever do anything in life, try to do it along the lines of "Brother" Pat Withrow."

"So – I had a dream."

Jones would see this dream come to fruition-- first in Florida, then later in his adopted hometown of Clintonville in rural Greenbrier County.

"I couldn't understand why some people were mean to us and others would give us food," he said. "Grandma and grandpa would sit me down and talk to me about it."

They would say, "Now, this is how it works. God chooses some people to do that kind of work, to give people stuff. Something happens to people in life that they want to be mean to us. Don't hold it against them. Always think on the good things."

"That is what they told us, which is that God will look out for us. We were sort of religious (Baptists), like most were where we lived."

A GUITAR, A BIBLE, AND A SHOTGUN

CHAPTER 17
SALVATION, EVEN FOR THE ANIMALS

In the spiritual side of life, Jones can find one avenue of laughter with regard to George. It occurred on the occasion of a revival the church was having, when one night, Jones and faithful ally, George, were taking it all in from a vantage point along a railroad track.

"We used to go to tent meetings, go sing and shout with them, just being a kid, you know," he recalled. "Back then, a kid could walk wherever he wanted to. It wasn't like it is today. This was in the summer time, and you know how long the daylight hours were. We walked down there and they were shouting and praising the Lord and everything. We were just sitting on that railroad track, listening to the singing.

"Well, we sat on the track, George and me, and we started shouting and hollering, doing the same things they were doing in the church. We started going back up the railroad track and grandma heard us coming. I was hollering and George was barking."

Grandma came out to us and asked, "What in the world is going on, Tommy?"

"Grandma, me and George got saved."

"Saved from what?" asked my puzzled grandmother.

"We just got saved at church. Hallelujah!"

"Did they baptize you?"

"No, we were out on the railroad track."

For the duration of the revival, Jones and George were mainstays. It was then, in his ninth year, that Jones felt a need to bring others into the spiritual fold, but he wasn't about to try his hand at preaching to any fellow humans.

Instead, he tried out his newfound evangelical talents on the animal world.

"George and me went around saving the chickens, the geese, everything we could find," he said.

His grandmother did nothing to discourage him, perhaps harboring a thought that her grandson might ultimately find his path that would lead him to the one he would pursue in adulthood.

More than one adult suggested that Jones set his sights on becoming a preacher, but Jones realized early on that that was not the life for him.

A GUITAR, A BIBLE, AND A SHOTGUN

"I was invited one time to speak at a place with a lot of people, but I just told them I couldn't handle that. I'm not a speaker but I believe in God very much."

Jones' turbulent life took another direction in the fifth grade when he was about fifteen years old and lagging far behind his peers. He decided to hang up his scholastic pursuits.

"I wasn't going to school anyway," he said. "I stayed in the woods a lot of the time; just me and the dogs. The truant officers got tired of fooling with us. So, I hid in the woods; the dogs would always give me away."

Grandma would say, "I wonder if Tommy went to school today."

"She'd look around and see that the dogs were gone and she knew I didn't go to school that day because me and the dogs were in the woods," he continued with a grin.

Jones didn't waste the hours away totally in youthful pursuits, however.

"I'd gather moss out of the woods," he said. "Got a quarter a sack. I just couldn't go to school. It was too rough."

Jones had no misgivings about his teachers but simply couldn't deal with the mental and physical abuse imposed by classmates.

For some reason unknown to him, the teachers didn't intervene and deal with the bullying by his schoolmates.

"I don't know why they were like that," he said. "A lot of them were kids just like me from families who had little money. We banded together when we moved to Quinwood."

Before they moved on to Quinwood, the old coal company house mysteriously burned to the ground in the little hamlet known as Vaughan.

"It just caught on fire one night," Jones remembers. "My sister and I got out and had nothing on but our nightclothes. The house was falling in. It burned up my bicycle, the brand new one that my mother had sent me. She did a lot of good for us later on."

No one was ever sure if the fire had been the handiwork of an arsonist but many folks in the community suspected that to be the case. Very few of the old coal houses were standing at the time in the late 1940's. Many had fallen victim to fire or simply collapsed under the weight of years of use and general disrepair.

"There are very few of them left," Jones said.

He paused and took a deep breath before continuing on with his recollections.

A GUITAR, A BIBLE, AND A SHOTGUN

"Grandpa worked at the sawmill at that time. He was a good carpenter, too. He even worked on the church for the people when they needed him. His nephew was a deacon, but they still weren't too good to us. I don't guess I'll ever understand why."

A friend of his grandfather owned a tool shed and, since the family had no place to call home after the fire had destroyed the ancient house, the friend cleaned out the structure and invited the family to convert it into a house. The man owned and lived in a small shanty about forty feet from the tool shed. We elected to take up residence in the tool shed.

"It was sort of embarrassing, but it was home," he said.

By this time, Jones' mother had married so the family picked up stakes and resettled in the Greenbrier County town of Quinwood.

"The guy she married was a good worker, but he was a drunkard and he gambled," Jones remembers. He was abusive to us. We didn't stay around him much. We'd see him and do what we had to do; but, he was mean to us - physically mean."

At times, the stepfather was not above striking the children.

"He hit us with whatever he had," Jones said. "If he was drunk, we just had to stay out of his way. We didn't live around him. I had an uncle who was the same way. They were just too evil to us and that bore on my mind. Anyway, my mom bought this old place and they were fixing it up."

Before long, his stepfather established a reputation as a solid worker and some invited him to buy the older houses with an eye toward repairing them for profit.

His mother picked out a house near a slate dump.

"It was down in colored town," Jones said. "She bought that house for two hundred dollars, the house and the lot. Then, she wrote us a letter telling us she got us a house and she wanted us to come to Quinwood."

So, with the aid of a man known only as Shorty, who arrived with his pickup truck to facilitate the move, the family was about to plant new roots.

"Grandpa fixed that house up in colored town and that's where we lived," Jones said. "That's where they first started calling me by the "N" word, but in the other town it was always "wop" and "grease ball". They still do that today along with other not too nice names like that."

Jones still wasn't sure if the Sicilian he came to learn about was his biological father.

"If it was him, I'm proud," he said. "If it wasn't him, I'm still proud."

Grandfather Bratton Jones pitched in using his experience at a saw mill to restore the old house so that it was livable.

"That's where we lived," Jones said. "We had some great black friends and we had some great white friends. We didn't know what it meant to have that many friends when we came to Quinwood. We never had so many friends like that except when we lived in Campbell's Creek in Kanawha County."

Even so, Jones was growing increasingly restless in school even though to this day he credits his efforts solely to his teachers.

"They had threatened to put grandma in jail, but I still didn't want to go to school," he said.

Mrs. Broughman did all she could to keep Jones in class, even warning that she personally would intervene and come after him if he refused to attend school.

"All the teachers were good to me," he said. "I just couldn't go to school because of the kids and the neighbors. When we got to Greenbrier County, we had some kin in the area. Others knew who we were. They were waiting for us and gave us a rough time. But we banded together, some of us poor kids.

"Brenda was a good-looking kid. Buddy, my half-brother, was with mom. He had been born in the same house and moved to Greenbrier County with us. He was one of the best car mechanics I've ever known in my life. I tell you what, I say this without bragging, that he could have worked on a NASCAR team. He was that good. He was gifted. People came from everywhere to get him to work on their cars."

Another teacher, known only as Mrs. Hayes, likewise did her best to inspire Jones to make something of himself academically by telling him at one stage, "Tommy, I'm going to tell you, you'd be an "A" student if you'd come to school. You just don't want to learn. Why don't you want to mix with other people?"

"Other people are cruel," Tommy answered in a whisper for no one to hear but him.

CHAPTER 18
GOOD FRIENDS AND BAD FRIENDS

Tommy tells us - we had a family friend in Quinwood whose name was Roger McDaniels. He would come to our home to sit and talk with us for hours. We went to a lot of places and Roger would travel with us. He would even go ramp digging with us.

A ramp is a lot like a wild onion but a whole lot stronger. We all love ramps in these mountains. Spring time is ramp digging time.

When Roger was younger, he had something wrong with him. I don't know what it was, but he walked on crutches for a long time. He was a few years younger than all of us.

Another friend of ours was Ray. Ray, Roger, and I were really good friends.

One day we were sitting around just talking about what we wanted to do in life. Roger said Ray and I would probably die in Quinwood, but Roger said he wouldn't.

Roger joined the Army and was sent to Vietnam. There was a truck load of troops and they ran over a land mine. Roger was the only one who was killed. He was right. He didn't die in Quinwood.

I remember when Roger would go out with us riding around. Sometimes we would go to car shows or go watch drag racing.

Ray was like me. We both went to work in the coal mines. Ray came to see me about two weeks before he got killed. He was an electrician in the mines. The power was supposed to be off, but it was on and he didn't know it was on. He was electrocuted. The day he came out to see me we really had a good time talking about the good old days. We remembered when we were growing up together in Quinwood and when we worked together in the mines.

His mother brought me his mining hat, mining belts, and boots he had on when he was electrocuted. I hung them up in my garage and I remember him every time I see them. He was a good friend.

It really was a big shock to me when Sharon and I, along with the girls, went to see my mother one evening and she told me that Ray had been electrocuted at work that day and killed in the mines. I was really shocked. I had seen him just two weeks earlier.

The evening that they were going to have his wake, Sharon and I went down to the funeral home in Rainelle early and asked them if we could see Ray. They said yes, so Sharon and I went in and told Ray good-bye.

I had another good friend in the late 1960's. His name was Bob Brewbaker. He was older than me. He was a really nice guy. He was in a really bad slate fall and there was no insurance or workman's compensation.

He worked for Skinny Campbell in a punch mine at Clerco.

He was in the hospital at Greenbrier Valley Hospital in Ronceverte for about three days and they said he had a heart attack. He was mashed up pretty bad. His brother had to come in from out of state to make all of the arrangements and pay everything.

There was a big guy named Junior and he had been drinking all day. He was drunk. Bob had consumed a few beers, too, but he wasn't drunk. We stopped on the way to Rupert where Bob bought a six pack of beer.

We were just a bunch of miners having a small meeting. We were standing around talking about coal production and whether or not we would get our payday.

Well, this Junior guy had been picking on Bob for a few weeks. Junior came up to Bob and was trying to start another fight with him. I just reached into the car and got one of Bob's beer cans. I was holding it when Junior went to hit Bob. I told him that he had better get on down the road.

Junior turned around like he was getting ready to leave. Junior bent over and picked up a rock and started walking away. He got about three or four feet away when he turned around and before he could throw the rock at Bob, I threw the beer can at him and hit him right between the eyes with it. When the can hit him, it busted. Beer went all over Junior and he fell forward in the dust. When he fell down, he started hollering that he was going to kill us all. At about the same time of the hollering, a police car pulled up. Junior was getting up. He had beer and dust all over him. He was an awful sight. The police put him in their car and told him that he was going with them. From that day onward, Junior wouldn't even speak to Bob.

When I was in the fourth grade, I had two good friends.

The girl's name was Dolly. She could sing really well and she would help me a lot with my lessons in school. She was like a sister to me.

The boy's name was Teddy. He was a real good friend. We palled around together all of the time.

They were both really good to me and my sister, Brenda.

It was good to have friends.

CHAPTER 19
THE BLUES

Tommy continues regaling us with his life tales. During my teenage years, anywhere from fifteen to seventeen years old, I played guitar a lot. Everyone thought that I would go professional. I'm not bragging, but everyone said I was really good.

When we lived down next to Charleston, we would hear the blues a lot. I loved the blues music there but when I came to Greenbrier County, I learned to sing the blues in the coal mines working with some colored men.

Then I started playing the blues a lot at home on the guitar. Blues was my favorite music, but most of the people I knew that played guitar didn't like blues, so I didn't play the blues around them.

I'm not a singer by any means. I cannot sing but I have always loved blues music. I always wanted to be a blues guitar player.

My first guitar only had three strings on it and one day I got a fourth string for it. That was when I started playing guitar more. Later on, I got quite a few really good guitars.

A GUITAR, A BIBLE, AND A SHOTGUN

When I was seventeen, I sent a tape to Mississippi to a blues festival. It was a reel to reel tape. That tells you it was a long time ago. They invited me to the blues festival. They had one every year. They said I was good and to come on down. I could cross the same stage that some the greats had played on, such as John J. Hooker, Gatemouth Brown, B.B. King, and many more.

I wish I had gone. Who knows? I could have been a great blues player today.

I guess it wasn't meant to be.

CHAPTER 20
LEAVING SCHOOL BEHIND
FOR GOOD

Jones was promoted to the sixth grade and it was then his life reached another one of those forks in the road, as far as attending classes was concerned.

"I had a mean teacher then who was sort of a big wheel in school. I just quit going to school," he said. "They had to run me through the woods. That was the life I was living."

All the while, racing in the back of his mind, was a thought that he would like to return the kindness that the Union Mission in Charleston had exhibited him a few years earlier.

"I wanted to have my own mission-- a food bank distributing food to the poor," he said. "A lot of people asked me why I didn't want to become a preacher. I had seen a lot of things out of preachers that weren't so good. I don't mean to throw off on them, but not all preachers practice what they preach.

"There was a girl in town that played marbles. Her name was Lois Jean. She was our friend. Her family was good to us. She became the marbles champion of West Virginia."

A GUITAR, A BIBLE, AND A SHOTGUN

Much of what Jones absorbed academically came at the hand of his grandfather.

"Grandpa taught me to read and write," he said. "He was like a school teacher. Grandma was almost totally illiterate. She could barely write her name."

Jones attended about two weeks of the sixth grade and decided then it was time to leave for good.

For some time, he had delivered the Charleston Daily Mail to earn some pocket change. Then he started picking up odd jobs around the mines. There were also some occasional excursions into the forests to gather moss.

"On Sundays, I had to make two trips to get all of the papers delivered," he said. "I had a bicycle, but I couldn't use it to deliver them up and down hollers because of the condition of the roads. I also delivered the Beckley newspaper when the regular guy was off."

In the mines, Jones was starting to learn a lifelong trade, cleaning out ditches and things of that nature to familiarize himself with the occupation of the coal industry.

Before that, he, at times, supplemented his meager income by picking and selling cherries and apples.

By the age of sixteen, he was working inside a coal mine, one of those "punch" mines or "wheelbarrow" mines that were prevalent in the area.

"I learned to do it all," he said. "It was a small mine to start with, a wheelbarrow mine. I worked at the one and even had a pony and a mule to work with. That was when they pulled pillars in the old works to recover the coal."

Jones was a tall, lanky sort and people just assumed he was older than his real age. From the wheelbarrow setups, he advanced to small coal mines using buggies and shooting coal with the aid of a continuous miner. The job was risky at all times evidenced, in his case, by breaking both hands.

His life took another detour in 1975 when he suffered a serious injury after a cable snapped on a continuous miner.

"The thing just snapped and flew and hit me on the side of the head," Jones said. "That thing busted my mining cap and put a big knot on my head. It put one little cut piece on my ear. Knocked me out cold. Blood was running over me. I fell down holding my head. They thought I was dead. My cap was laying there broken into two pieces. The blood was caused by a cut place and it was running in my ear. I still have a little trouble on that side."

For Jones, it meant a career in the mines was coming to a rapid halt after sixteen years.

Jones held a succession of jobs mostly in Greenbrier County in the little punch mines as the workers referred to them.

Some of the bosses were top-notch, such as Chester Odell. Others refused, at times, to pay him his wages. He made the circuit, working coal mines in Anjean, Muddlety in the Summersville area, and even in the town of Mullens in Wyoming County.

"No matter where I'd go, I could get a job at those punch mines," he said.

It was at a coal mine in Beckley that his career came to a complete and total end with the accident that nearly took his life.

"I got covered with coal on that conveyor belt," he said. "It pushed my nose right down. I was laying down flat in about thirty inches of coal. They were trying to start the belt. When it started, it pushed me right down and burned some of the hide right off me. The coal and mud stuck in my face. It didn't break my back, but it certainly stretched it out. I spent eleven days in a hospital in Clifton Forge, Virginia, at the old C & O Hospital. I've never been what you would call stout in my back any more. I used to be pretty doggone stout in the back."

For a while, Jones received some Worker's Compensation for his injury he suffered in an accident that left him totally covered by coal.

"All I had was my arm and head sticking out," he recalled. "That was it. It was just goosing along the belt, because they were doing it by remote control. Me and another guy were putting the belt back in there. It had to be done that night. They told us this beltline had to be ready for the day shift. That was a union mine. If you were a certified miner, they could make you do anything. I wasn't scared of dying. I was just worried about other things. A lot of things were crossing my mind. That belt would stop and then start again. They knew we were down there but didn't know where we were at. There was maybe five hundred feet of belt or more."

Tommy's coworker managed to get out of harm's way and pulled Tommy by a leg to get him out from underneath the huge pile of coal.

"If he hadn't been there, I would have smothered to death," Jones figures. "It did burn some hide off my back. I still have trouble with a leg when I'm walking. I can get around. I think that the worst thing in my life was when I got hit in the head the other time. I'm absent-minded a lot these days. I'm tone deaf. The cable was on the old continuous miner. The cable is actually what hit me. The cable was pretty good sized. It was a steel cable as big around as your thumb."

Jones was hurt in a mine that was operating under Grandview near Beckley in some of the more rugged terrain east of the Mississippi River.

"There were several mines up there at different times," he said. "It was not a good place to work."

On another occasion, a slab of slate dropped onto his right foot breaking it while he was working in a Charmco area mine in Greenbrier County.

"A big knot is still on that foot today," he said. "I have to wear two sizes of shoes. I buy two pairs at once, each pair a different size. Usually I get them at flea markets. I normally wear a size ten, but I have to also get a size eleven. I can wear a ten if it doesn't lace up. I've got cowboy boots, but I can't wear them because of the knot on my foot."

CHAPTER 21
WHILE HIS GUITAR GENTLY WEEPS

Losing his sense of musical tones was especially difficult for Tommy to accept. That meant he no longer could play the guitar, an avocation in earlier years that allowed him to earn a few bucks by sitting in on some gigs within his circle of friends.

"I was self-taught," he says proudly when talking about his accomplishment.

His grandmother had purchased him an inexpensive guitar, one that featured a photograph of the singing cowboy himself, Gene Autry, and his faithful horse, Champion.

Mrs. Jones had managed to find a bargain on another guitar since it had been used by a neighbor's son for his introduction into music.

"I did pretty good on it," Jones said. "Then I went on to better guitars and used to sit in with other bands. Most of this happened in Kanawha County. I'd go back and sit in with a band at Joyland, an amusement park. It was a continuous thing in the summer time. That was down around Belle, if I remember right."

This was when he was around fifteen to seventeen years old, and for Jones, it meant not only some moments of pleasure but opportunities to put a little folding money in his wallet.

"We'd go on and on," he said. "I learned what we called "hot licks" and some people thought I was pretty good. Maybe I really wasn't any better or as good as some of the other kids."

At no time did Jones add any vocalization to his guitar playing explaining simply that he wasn't a singer.

"I had a different style of playing," he said. "Blues was what I loved but I liked country and rock'n'roll. I met Joe Maphus, one time, the guitar player from California. He walked out of where he was playing and talked to us. I kept my eye on that guitar of his. He was doing a thing for the Fourth of July. He was a real nice person."

Jones would lend his talents to any of the honky-tonks that dotted the West Virginia landscapes.

"I never played in any of the beer joints," he said. "I don't know why. I guess it was because I wasn't a drinker."

When he remarried, his first wife donated a car and some furniture to the couple. The three of them remain in touch.

CHAPTER 22
HIS OWN MISSION

Five years before the life-changing mishap at the Beckley mines, Jones and his second wife headed for Florida when he was between mining jobs.

He drove a produce truck, hauling mostly celery on the edge of the Everglades, in a place known as Lake Okeechobee.

"I hauled it from packing house to packing house in a small truck that was only about a ton and a half," he said. "Sharon worked there, too, on the inside packing the stuff. I liked the job, but we wouldn't make enough money to live there. I saw all this food that we could get and went looking at all of the empty buildings. I began to think that I would like to start a mission there. I couldn't make enough money. I could have done it if I could have made enough money. I knew how to get the food because they would give it to you."

Leftover vegetables were dumped in a field and other trucks would come in and saturate it with diesel fuel and burn it up.

"There would be these migrant workers out there and they didn't have much to eat," he said. "So, I would take what was left out there and give it to them."

A GUITAR, A BIBLE, AND A SHOTGUN

The boss told me, "If they need it, if they're hungry, give it to them but tell them they can't sell it."

Jones knew that donated vegetables his employer couldn't sell were not being sold, in turn, by the migrants.

"They were hungry," he said. "Sharon would go with me. A couple of times, she even drove the small truck. Anyhow, these guys came up to me and this is something that brings tears to my eyes. These guys were right there when I worked, loading, watching a pre-cooler, getting it ready to ship out. I had stocked some corn on the dock."

Standing just a short distance away were some prisoners; their every movement scrutinized by a shotgun-toting guard.

"They all kept looking at me," Jones said. "This one guy was talking to the guard, and I thought, this would be a rough way to make it. You have to be in jail and then would have to get out here and work."

One of the younger inmates approached Jones and asked, "Could me and my fellow inmates here have some of that corn since you're going to throw it out? We'd like to take it out to the jail tonight for supper," the young man explained.

Jones immediately went to see his boss to explain the situation and his employer assured him, "Yeah, give them all they want. Tell then they can go out to the dump and get it."

Jones was about fifty feet away from the toiling inmates. He got down off the dock and approached the guard.

"Can they come up here and talk to me?"

Not once did the guard say anything to him but a Cuban in the crowd who spoke fluent English opened a conversation with him.

"You know," he told Jones. "We're not violent. We're just out here working. I'm in jail for non-support. I couldn't feed my family. That's why I'm in jail."

"That brought tears to my eyes," Jones said in recalling the incident. "We were bowing our heads to keep others from seeing us cry. They were telling me their stories. They said they had to work off fines and stuff like that. That is why they wanted a handout of corn that was destined for the trash dump."

"Any time you see me, I'll give you some food," Jones promised the big Cuban. "I looked up at this big black guy. We were all bawling. I couldn't see through my tears. He looked like a basketball player. He was crying so much the tears were running from his eyes like a waterfall. He was so happy to get that food."

At that point, Jones turned to his wife and remarked, "That's why I'd like to start this mission down here."

"I just couldn't do it there," he said. "I really wanted to do it, but I couldn't make enough to live on. We lived there several months. You didn't get steady hours there. You'd work sixteen hours one day and two hours the next."

This was in 1970, five years before the mining accident, and his daughter was only one month old.

"They've got a lot of mean people down there, too," he said.

Once he quit the mines for good, Jones and his wife, Sharon, turned almost exclusively to recycling and performing odd jobs to keep the bills paid and food on the table. Before long, Jones would realize a boyhood dream and start the process for getting food into the hands of the needy, the working poor, and the elderly with no means to sustain themselves.

"I did go on to have the biggest food bank in Greenbrier County," he said. "That was my dream."

For a long time, the couple recycled every discarded item that was worth the effort.

"Anything, like cans, right on up to car parts," he said.

When they first opened shop, the two innocently ran afoul of the law, unaware that they were supposed to have obtained a special license before getting into that type of enterprise.

"We traded cars," he said. "We loved cars. We weren't selling cars. We were just taking parts off and selling the parts, not the cars. We did high performance. This wasn't a business, but they made us quit. We had a couple of '69 Corvettes. They were not road-worthy. We would always trade off cars before we got them completely fixed."

Just about anything that could be sold and donated passed through the Jones' place, right into the hands of the people who had been victimized by just about any imaginable tragedy, such as flooding, hurricanes, and tornadoes.

"And how was I making it?" he asked, and then answered. "When I got hurt, I received a small settlement from Workmen's Compensation and we recycled everything we could to help us buy food and pay bills. My mom would help when she could. So, I thought I could get out and make it, and I did."

Then, up until his retirement, Jones turned to Social Security for a disability payment.

"Now, all I get is regular Social Security," he said. "No miner's pension. No black lung."

Jones says he attempted to secure a license for a salvage yard but was turned down.

"The law says if you live within a certain distance of a dwelling, you can't have a salvage yard, not within so many feet of a hard-top road," he said. "We could have had a big salvage yard there, but we couldn't do it because we couldn't get a license. So, we had to give it up."

Everyone, or so it seemed to Jones, was in the business of selling car parts.

"We didn't make much money and we donated what we had from it," he said.

Anytime the couple accepted canned food, they insisted on a receipt, after issuing explicit directions as to where it should end up in his mission.

"We gave everything away from recycling," Jones said. "It's hard to do, but we did it. We donated to charities as far away as a mission in California. We donated to a Sioux Indian reservation in South Dakota."

There have been times when unscrupulous folks have sought to exploit his generosity and Jones can vividly recall such times and the people involved.

"People thought I was soft-hearted and a lot of people came and tried to buy stuff from us," he said. "We had a little piece of land, and one man came by one day and said I'll give you a certain amount for that little piece of land."

Jones would have none of the man's feeble offer to separate him and the little plot of earth.

"Look," he told the would-be purchaser, "I'm soft-hearted but I'm not that soft-hearted."

Nor soft-headed as things turned out.

Fellow humans weren't exclusively objects of their efforts, either.

Jones carried the memory of his faithful George right into middle-age and that part explains why he and his wife are so fond of animals.

"We work for animals, too," he said. "We even sent things for an animal shelter in Pahokee, Florida. We had wanted to start a mission there after seeing the migrant workers-- the people we had given the vegetables to."

When we lived in Florida, we had an opportunity to help a different kind of animal. We were driving home from work one day and we spotted a big alligator going across the road a few yards in front of us. We slowed down and came to a complete stop. We watched a baby alligator come up onto the road.

"I pulled over to the center of the road so people would stop. Sharon and I got out of our vehicle. We found a stick and kept pushing the little gator across the road. It took us a while and we had to keep watching for his mom. She moved on and when we got the baby gator across the road, it saw its mom and scurried into the canal to be near her. When we got back into the car, there were quite a few cars on both sides of the road. We drove off like nothing happened. Some people gave us the thumbs up sign and hollered 'well done'; others were mad, but we didn't care. We saved the baby's life and that's all that mattered to us."

Linda Hudson Hoagland

CHAPTER 23
DON'T LET YOUR BABIES GROW UP TO BE COWBOYS

One thing Jones definitely wasn't cut out to be in following the various paths in his life was to work as a performer in the all-American rodeo. He had come dangerously close once to doing just that with an event that called for him to ride a Brahma bull.

Jones was trying to earn some folding money as a handyman on an authentic ranch in Texas, in Odessa, near Midland, in the early 1960's, hoping to land something a little more profitable and permanent.

"I wasn't a drifter. I was just down there looking for a job," he said.

So, he wound up on a ranch helping haul hay and other feed, working alongside the son of the owner. Not too long after finishing some back-breaking work at the ranch, Jones had seen more than his fill of the life of a cowhand.

"I'm going home," he told the owner's son, who was himself a champion bull rider. "I appreciate the job on this ranch, but it's not me."

One day as the two were pitching hay, the son announced his intentions to take him down to the site of the rodeo where animals are trained for show purposes.

"You just don't go out and get wild bulls and turn them loose in the rodeo," Jones said. "You have to know how to get them to come out of the chute. I went with him and people thought I was a bull rider. I didn't tell them any differently. Man, they were really nice to me, patting me on the back, so I let them believe I was a bull rider. I looked at it this way, how many people haul a bull around just to see if you can ride it in the parking lot? They had this big bull and they thought we were there to train it."

As he inched closer to the ring, however, Jones began to acquire a sudden sense of reality, not to mention a quick case of cold feet.

"I looked just like a cowboy and I had been working on a ranch, so I was sort of a cowboy," he said. "But I was just working for enough gas money to get back home. Anyhow, I walked up there. I was so nervous."

Climbing up the wooden chute area, he looked down on the ornery creature beneath him and knew this wasn't his line of work.

The bull was more than ready but Jones wasn't. The only thing moving in him or on him were his bowels and bladder.

That's right – nature was taking its course without any direct help from Tommy.

"Is all that coming from the bull?" one veteran cowboy inquired as he looked at a widening puddle on the ground.

"No, it's coming from me. The bull hasn't even started yet."

I had to put my knees together to reach the bathroom.

That was the extremely short cowboy career of one Tommy Jones.

"They never asked me anything, but I was ready to tell them. Hey, that bull ain't wild enough for me. I got a kick out of that."

CHAPTER 24
FRED

One time, a small red dog came to our house in Clintonville. He was a real smart little guy. We called him Fred. He was really a cute little dog.

I was usually outside most of the time working on one vehicle or another. I had quite a few of them back then.

Fred loved to play a lot and one day I was playing with him in the front yard. I got up to go into the house and I told Fred, "Why don't you make yourself useful and go get our paper?"

We would get a free paper twice a week, one on Wednesday evening and another on the weekend.

Well, if it has been raining or rained the day before, or snowing, they roll the paper up and slide it into a blue plastic bag.

It just so happened that the day before, it had rained, so they had the papers in a blue plastic bag. I went into the house to eat and rest a while. About an hour and a half later, I went back out the kitchen door through the garage.

When I looked up there laid Fred under a big pine tree in front of our garage. There were a lot of blue plastic bags lying all around him under the pine tree. Not only did he get our paper, he also went all over the neighborhood and got all the neighbor's papers, too.

I looked down at him and I could swear that he was smiling at me as if to say, "Well, I went and got all of your papers so where is my treat?"

CHAPTER 25
UNCLE JESSE

One time, Sharon and I heard that the old white-haired man that played Uncle Jesse on the Dukes of Hazzard was going to be at a department store in Fairlea. He was promoting something for the store.

He had two women with him. We were told that one was his wife and the other was his manager.

We got into line with about nine other people. There weren't that many in line. We watched him as we went down the line.

He was really nice to the well to do people. They were real dressed up with big rings on, but when it came to the working-class people, he tried to rush us all through as fast as he could. He was signing black and white pictures for one dollar each.

We just went over there because we thought that the General Lee car would be there, too. At that time, we had a Dodge Charger just like the General Lee except that ours was white. The car wasn't there.

When we got up to Uncle Jesse, he misspelled Sharon's name. He grabbed up the picture and tore it in two and threw it into the trash can. They were all up on a little platform that had been built for them to sit on.

When he tore the picture, the woman on his right said, "Well, there goes another dollar."

Uncle Jesse was really arrogant and rude after I got my picture.

I told him what kind of actor I thought he was and how arrogant and rude he was. As we walked down the platform, I started to hold up my index finger and instead I held up my middle finger. His eyes bulged out and his face turned really red. Someone hollered for security, but we walked on into the store and did a little shopping.

I don't think they had security at the store.

We went out and got into our Charger and left two black streaks on the pavement in the parking lot. Sharon was driving.

CHAPTER 26
SHARON'S FIRSTS

I bought Sharon her first car. It was only two years old when I bought it in 1975. It was a 1973 Dodge Challenger, 340 engine, 4-speed. It was metal flake blue with a black vinyl roof. It was a really nice car.

We lived in Rainelle, then. Right after that we moved to Clintonville where we had a lot of cars. We traded a lot of cars back then. We eventually ended up with two more Challengers. Sometimes we would trade one car for maybe two or three and sometimes we would trade two or three for one.

We had so many cars that I can't even remember them all. I would fix them up some and then I would trade them off. We never sold any, we would always trade them.

I just loved cars.

I also bought Sharon her first bicycle. When she was a kid, she never did own a bicycle. So, I bought her one. We both have one, but we never ride them anymore, too many years have piled on.

I also bought her a 1981 Firebird that she still owns.

CHAPTER 27
PEOPLE JUDGING OTHER PEOPLE

I was affiliated with some Jehovah Witnesses for a while quite a few years ago. When we started the food bank, rumors started flying that we were Jehovah Witnesses. We had had trouble with people thinking that we were Jehovah Witnesses for quite a few years, even before we ever moved to Clintonville. Every time we would go to a store, nine times out of ten, there would be a neighbor of ours working there. They harass you if they think you are a Jehovah Witness. No matter what your religion is, no one should condemn you for what they think you are. This has happened for a lot of years. I wonder if any one of these people have ever walked in any one else's shoes, or if they would do it if they could get a chance to do so.

When we go into a bank, we are harassed a lot. We have a neighbor that went to work at the same bank we banked at. So, now when we make a payment, we have to mail it. It's a real eye opener when they think you are a Jehovah Witness.

One time at the food bank, I was beaten up in our front yard because they thought that I was a Jehovah Witness.

On April 13, 1996, we were being harassed by some neighbors and when the law came out, they jumped on me. Within an hour, I was in the Intensive Care Unit at Greenbrier Valley Hospital in Ronceverte with a heart attack. All of those medical bills, I still owe. Medicare paid some of it and now I'm responsible for the rest. I don't have any money to pay on them. We live on a fixed income and most of my Social Security I get is usually gone (paying bills) by the time I get it.

It is just plain wrong the way people treat you when they think you are one thing when you are not. In some of the stores where we shop, some of the people will follow us out of the store to the parking lot and want to fight me because they think I'm a Jehovah Witness.

I am not a Jehovah Witness.

If your skin isn't the right color or you are not their religion, or if that doesn't work, they call you gay.

"My question is, who are they to criticize others?"

I have always noticed that the people that are out there hollering and talking against others are the ones that have something to hide.

Like the young boy, Mathew Shepherd, that lived in the Midwest. Some boys hung him and tied him to a fence. They beat him really bad until he was dead. I think they got some prison time but I'm not sure how much. This happened all because he was gay.

There was a girl down next to Charleston when I was a teenager. She was sort of poor, but she was a really pretty girl. All because she was shy and stayed to herself, the other teens always picked on her and called her gay and other names all of the time. One day she had had enough. She killed herself.

I grew up with a boy down next to Charleston. When his son was a teenager, everyone picked on him and called him gay. One day, he couldn't take any more, so he shot and killed himself. He was a straight A student.

I learned one thing through all of this. Those who are speaking out the most and the loudest are usually the ones that have something to hide.

CHAPTER 28
TOMMY'S HEART ATTACK

On April 13, 1996, there was a bunch of punks and men running up and down the road hollering and yelling. When they were below our house, they started barking and yelling just to excite our dogs making them bark.

I walked into the house and called the deputy sheriff's office in Rupert. Deputy Hinkley told me, "I patrol that road all of the time."

"I have never seen any law patrolling this road," I answered back.

I don't think he liked that very well.

His next words were, "I'm really looking forward to meeting you, Mr. Jones."

You can see the top of the road from our yard. I saw the deputy racing down the hill really fast. He drove up into our yard.

I was standing about four feet from the door.

He threw his door open, stuck his foot up on the frame, and just sat there.

I saw a tape recorder beside his leg.

About that time, a state police car came down the hill and pulled in behind Deputy Hinkley. The state police officer's name was John Rapp. Officer Rapp got out of his car and stood beside Hinkley's Jeep next to the door behind the driver's door. He held his hand over his gun all the time he was standing there.

"What's going on?" asked Deputy Hinkley.

"We have some neighbors going up and down the road cursing and hollering and calling us dirty names. After they get below our driveway, they would yell and bark like dogs just to get our dogs to barking. This isn't the first time," I explained.

Both men acted real hostile towards me.

"Go around the hill and talk to the man who done it," Deputy Hinkley told Officer Rapp.

I never once thought that I would call the law about people harassing us and the police would come to our home and start jumping on me.

It was just a little while after they left that I started having bad chest pains. I drove myself to the hospital in Fairlea. I was throwing up all the way over there.

"You've had a heart attack," they told me and put me in ICU for two days and one night. Then they transferred me upstairs for one night telling me that I had a small heart attack,

If that was a small one, I sure don't want to have a large one.

I was afraid to call 9-1-1 because I was afraid the ones who had been harassing me would hear it on the scanner and come back to jump on Sharon or stop me on the way over there, maybe even kill me. They thought that I was a Jehovah Witness because at one time I was affiliated with them.

CHAPTER 29
DONATING FOR SCIENCE

I donated my body to science at WVSOM (West Virginia School of Osteopathic Medicine) in Lewisburg. My donation is to help the students learn from my body and to help others in the future.

I donated my body in 1996. A couple of months later, Sharon donated her body.

My mother donated her body in 1997. She passed away December 13, 2003.

After the students finish learning all about your body and what all you had wrong with you, they cremate it.

My mother's ashes are at the Rosewood Mausoleum in Lewisburg.

Your family can take the ashes if that is your wish.

My half brother, Buddy, donated his body to the same school.

Sharon's sister, Mary Elizabeth, who lives in Upper Sandusky, Ohio, donated her body to a medical school in her area. She passed away Wednesday, May 13, 2009.

There were a few people that came to our food bank and pet food bank that we ran here at our home for quite a few years that wanted to know how to donate. We gave food out for the Union Mission in Charleston, West Virginia for three years. A portion of the food came from Larry and Francis Jones at Feed the Children in Oklahoma. We met a lot of people who needed help.

The people that came here and got food would ask us how we went about donating our bodies and we gave them the phone number and told them how to get information from the school.

Another reason we donated our bodies is because we can't afford to bury one another. When I became disabled in 1985, I signed up on Disability Social Security. That's when I found out that a lot of the little punch mines, nine out of ten, that I worked for that held out Social Security for me, never sent anything in to Social Security.

I worked hard all of my life just to have something for my family and me.

Some of those mines turned in a very meager amount; most of them didn't turn in anything at all.

I think there is something very wrong with our Social Security System.

CHAPTER 30
REMAINING MEMORIES BEFORE
HIS MIND FADED

I had a cousin who everyone called Uncle Joe Geradono. He was part Sicilian like me.

He met a woman in Charleston. Her name was Lucenda and Uncle Joe fell in love with her. He said that Lucenda and he were going to make marriage.

Uncle Joe Geradono drove a big, tandem coal truck. When he wasn't tasting moonshine, he would haul coal.

Everyone kept telling him that he didn't want to marry that woman, meaning Lucenda, because she had slept with every man in Charleston.

Uncle Joe would say, "Ha! Charleston no bigga place."

Uncle Joe's best friend was Ralph, who had only one leg. Ralph would tell everyone that the other leg was shot off in the war. The truth was that he had only one leg, because he was confronted by a woman's jealous husband. He was caught by her gun toting husband in bed making "whoopee" to the angry man's his wife. The wound was so bad that Ralph's leg had to be amputated and replaced with an artificial limb.

One day, Uncle Joe came home early and caught his good friend, Ralph, in bed with Lucenda, Uncle Joe's wife.

Ralph forgot about his artificial leg as he ran out the back door holding onto the walls to steady himself. He grabbed a broom to help him hobble into a big cornfield.

Lucenda ran out the front door and climbed up into a big apple tree in the front yard.

"Come on down, Lucenda," Uncle Joe told her.

"You're going to whip me, aren't you, Joe?" she said.

"Yep," he said as he turned around to go back into the house where he picked up his new "thaw." That's what he called his new chain saw.

He returned to the apple tree and proceeded to cut it down.

Lucenda rolled out of the tree and started running down the railroad track.

Uncle Joe Geradono didn't follow her. He just let her go.

Every day he sat on his front porch and cried.

Finally, a few neighbors went to talk to Uncle Joe Geradono.

They all told him, "Don't worry, Uncle Joe Geradono. Lucenda will come back."

He just looked at them and said, "The heck with Lucenda. Me want me apple tree back. Me love me apple tree."

I had a cousin who only had one eye. His damaged eye was put out by a lady who ran a dancing parlor in town. It was all over fifty cents.

The side and back doors of the dancing parlor were for influential people and well to do gentlemen.

Cousin Louie would go through the front door where he watched the money collectors charge the people that came through the back and side doors only fifty cents for a dance and beverage. He had to pay a dollar for the same dance and beverage.

Cousin Louie and the lady who owned the dance parlor got into an argument. The lady owner stabbed Louie in the eye with a pencil.

It blinded him for life and it was over fifty cents.

Cousin Louie said, "I wish I had my eye glasses on that day or I wish I had never learned to dance. I would still have both eyes."

When I was a kid, we lived up Campbell's Creek in a little coal company town called Cinco.

The coal dust on the road was called float dust. It was really thick most of the time except for when it rained. When you moved your feet, black dust would swirl around your feet. Every time a car would go by, you had to hold your hand over your mouth just to breathe.

The dogs that would go with us would start barking and chase the cars. When they came back to us, we couldn't see them until the dust settled.

A bunch of us kids would go to the company store almost every day, back then there was penny candy and soda pop.

There was boy that was overweight whose name was Bob. He had a big bandage on his foot. The bandage had turpentine on it. Bob couldn't walk on his sore foot, so he had to hop around on one foot.

I went next door and borrowed a wheelbarrow that had a metal wheel on it.

Since I was the tallest, they all elected me to push the wheelbarrow with Bob in it to the company store. I parked the wheelbarrow next to the company store porch.

Everyone who came out of the store asked us, "What happened to Bob's foot?"

"He stepped on a nail and can't walk," was what we told everyone who asked.

Everyone who walked by threw change (pennies, nickels, dimes, and quarters) into the wheelbarrow.

The other kids noticed Bob getting money so the next day those same kids went to the company store with bandages on their arms, hands, and feet.

The store manager came out and told them, "It's not nice to try to fool people into giving you money. Go on home and quit that."

When I grew up, I was always asked about the boys who would go to the company store with me, where they were, and what they did for a living.

Bob went on to be a banker. Pete went on to be a probation officer. Jim went into preaching. All of the other kids went on to do pretty well in life.

Me? Well - I'm still pushing the wheelbarrow.

Sharon and I had a really good friend by the name of Mary. She and her husband, Claude Jones, used to come out to the house any time we would call her to help us with our food bank.

Her husband, Claude, died in 2004 of lung cancer.

When Mary was younger, a teenager, she used to sing on WOAY Radio Station for the Reverend Mont Carr and the Reverend Freddy Steel.

She is real good looking and can sing well still yet.

She worked at the Tea Room in Charleston when she was young. She is and has always been a real good worker.

She has blonde hair and hazel eyes.

Everyone always said she should become a professional singer, but she never did.

Claude and I used to work in the coal mines together. Claude was a really good coal miner and a very hard worker.

Mary has been a really good friend of ours since 1996. That's when we started giving food out from the Union Mission from Charleston. We gave out food and pet food. We still have a small food bank where we give out food and pet food but in smaller amounts.

Our food bank got so large, at one time, that we were giving out food to four counties and some of it went out of state a few times.

We gave out coats every year. We would go to flea markets and yard sales to buy coats during the year and then we would give them out to our food bank. We also shipped them out to all kinds of missions across the United States.

The Rev. Rex Whiteman really helped us out a lot with the food bank. He was the CEO of the Union Mission. He and his wife, Kay, were some of the nicest and kindest people we have ever known.

Now we just give out mostly pet food.

We don't give any food out from the Union Mission any more. We haven't for a long time. We are just not able to do it anymore.

We will always give out pet food and coats.

One day, Sharon and I went to Monroe County to deliver some auto parts: about fifteen starters, twenty alternators, and miscellaneous parts.

Our truck was sitting in the yard with a flat tire, so we took the car. We were delivering the automobile parts to another salvage yard.

After we got there, the salvage workers came out to help us unload the car trunk and back seat.

Sharon and I left after the car was unloaded and as we drove home, we were talking. I wasn't really paying attention. We started around a curve, a right-hand curve, and I didn't slow down enough for the curve. Half way around the curve I was all the way on the other side of the road and I ran off the edge of the road onto the gravels.

A little bit past the curve, I managed to get the car back on the right side of the road. It scared us so bad. We were both white as ghosts and we didn't say a thing for a good while.

"What's that real awful smell?" Sharon asked.

I told her, "I don't know, but I think I'm sitting in it."

We had to drive the rest of the way home with the windows open wide.

The dogs and cats were really happy to see us when we pulled into the driveway but when we got out of the car, they backed up, and wouldn't come up to us or near the car.

I think they smelled that awful smell.

When I was a kid, I went to school with a girl that everyone called Smarty. Even the teachers called her Smarty because she was really smart.

You could ask her anything, like "What month and day does the 4th of July come on?" and she could answer it. "What month and day does Christmas come on," and she could answer really fast.

A GUITAR, A BIBLE, AND A SHOTGUN

Every time we would have a test, I would always copy off of Smarty's paper. I was really making good grades when I could get the chance to copy off of her.

One day we had a test and the teacher told me that she knew I was copying from Smarty. Here is how come I know. It seems that Smarty got every one of her answers right except for the last one and Tommy got all of his answers right except for last one. Smarty wrote on her paper, "I do not know the answer to this last one." Tommy wrote on his paper, "Me either."

CHAPTER 31
HELP FOR THE NEEDY

Jones found his niche in life in 1997 when be began distributing food in a major way. Long before the big change, he and his wife had been passing out food to the needy on a small scale, normally such staples as pork and beans, as well as some food for pets.

"We've been here thirty-three years now," he reflected. "When we first came out, we started giving out a little bit at a time. All of my life, I have been giving stuff away. When we gave out the pork and beans, it was from the back of our car, a Camaro."

Jones says he always bought the food he donated on those early beginnings since no one was providing any items at that time.

"My mom helped us," he said. "We picked out the people we knew who needed it badly. Old people. Hurt and sick people."

No one refused but a few felt it was some kind of gimmick setting them up for a rip-off.

"We didn't ask for any donations and we didn't get any," Jones recalled. "One poor old fellow sticks out in my mind. I offered to get him a bag of pet food."

"I'm not a Christian," he said.

"You don't have to be a Christian," Jones replied. "We love animals and we love people," he added.

Jones continued, "One Christmas, we gave out ten thousand pounds of stuff – five tons including pet food."

Then in 1997, Jones and his wife were the subjects of a newspaper article detailing their humanitarian efforts on behalf of the poor, far and wide, and things began to snowball.

No longer would this be a miniscule operation handled from the trunk of a car to the porch of a beneficiary.

Sharon Jones dispatched letters of inquiry to Union Mission, the same folks who had bailed her husband's family out of a few jams when he was a youngster, and the faith-based charity in Charleston responded in a huge way.

Its director, Rex Whiteman, began supplying the couple with truckloads of food items for distribution.

Jones said he often hands over what change is left when he shops at Kroger's to anyone out in the parking lot.

"I don't just single out people because they look poor," he said. "I came out of Kroger's in Fairlea and I had one dollar and some change left in my pocket. I told a guy out there that this is what I have left. I'm going to give it to you for good luck. I do people that way. If I have an extra dollar, I give it away but there's always somebody who thinks there's a catch to it. There is no catch. I hope they see that I'm as poor as they are and that they'll give a little to somebody else."

Jones says he was merely heeding the advice of Pat Withrow who often supplied the family with food and other items from the Union Mission back in his boyhood.

"I can see what it does for people. In my mind and heart is what my grandmother told me,' he says. "It's not for show. I've never tried to do that. If I was doing this for a profit or a show, I'd have more than what I've got. We make it. God has always provided us something to eat. It may not be a lot. Right today, I'll give people stuff. I'm not trying to be a braggart."

However, it seems some aren't convinced.

"People will say that I'm tooting my own horn and I say, well, you'd better stand back because I'm going to deafen you. That's the thanks you get from a lot of people," he said.

Rex Whiteman put the Jones into the major leagues of food distribution when he sent in a two-ton truck laden with a variety of staples. A portion came from Larry Jones (no relation) of Christian Television's "Feed the Children" based on Oklahoma.

"His ministry has really been good to us," he said.

By the middle of 2000, however, dark clouds had begun to appear on the couple's charity and they were forced to throw in the towel.

"There was a lot of controversy," he said. "People wanted food because they thought they could make money from it. They saw that we had all this food and it sort of irritated them. Some churches thought we were taking donations that were meant for them. We offered to give anything extra to them."

Someone used a gun to blast some windows out of the couple's food trailer. Police were called in, but no arrests were made. In the midst of this, Sharon Jones reached her flashpoint and tried to end her life with an overdose of prescription medicine.

With the food donated by Union Mission, the couple were keeping the needy supplied on the edge of four counties. The only rule the Charleston outfit insisted on was that religious services had to be conducted, so the couple began leading Bible studies on a non-denominational basis.

"We tried to cover everybody," Jones said. "We're not a name-brand religion – Baptist, Holiness, or anybody. I grew up around all of them. One man thought I was a Jehovah Witness and beat me up."

In the melee, Jones said he felt a deep pain in his chest and realized he had been stabbed with a sharp object.

"Police were summoned but never showed up," he said.

Jones said he never bothered to get a warrant because his assailant was a relative by marriage. At any rate, Jones said he suffered a black eye and damage to a set of false teeth which remain in a state of disrepair.

"He even kicked me in the leg," Jones recalled. "I'm not a fighter. I'm not a lover, either. I just try to help people. He did all the fighting. I was just holding him off. I went to see the prosecutor."

He just stood in the doorway and said, "Misdemeanor, misdemeanor, misdemeanor."

Which in effect meant it wasn't worth his time pursing, Jones reasoned.

In spite of such antics by a small minority of troublemakers, Jones said he might have continued with his food distribution effort but a man at the Union Mission in Charleston that worked in the warehouse said that he would rather give the food to a place in White Sulphur Springs or another food bank location.

I think it was because we weren't his religion. We were both Baptists.

Even so, the couple didn't completely get out the charity business.

"We still gather up food," Jones said. "We buy stuff on sale."

"We both love animals. We have a small animal rescue here at home. We call it "Second Chance Ranch". We have always taken care of animals and I figure we will until we are both gone," adds Sharon.

Of late, Jones has suffered a major health setback, developing prostate cancer, a common ailment of men in his generation.

"I believe in prayer and medicine," he said.

At one time, he and his wife boasted the largest food bank in Greenbrier County. While their operation has been scaled back, the two continue to round up soup and packages of noodles for older residents along with pet food when they can get it.

In the midst of the turmoil, jealousy from others veiled his success. One mean-spirited person broke into a trailer containing foodstuffs, opened huge cans of mustard and beans, and poured them across the floor and walls.

"We don't know why they did it," he said. "These people seemed to know when we were both gone. Now, one of us stays here all the time. Right today, we have to watch our place. They just didn't like us. They thought I was a Jehovah Witness. They called me a Seventh Day Adventist. They called me a Holy Roller."

Jones had a ready response for those brazenly displaying the ignorance of bigotry and intolerance.

"Are we not supposed to help everybody? Not just pick out one certain group. That has always been my belief. We're supposed to help anything and everybody."

Besides food stuffs, the couple shipped off as many coats and jackets as they could round up at flea markets over the years.

"I've been harassed all life," he said when asked to theorize why some people took such a violent reaction to his efforts on behalf of the needy. "I've been put down. When I went to school, I remember how some people treated me. You still see it today. You see kids pick on other kids. All this stuff and it still goes on in the schools.

A GUITAR, A BIBLE, AND A SHOTGUN

You should talk to people like me to see what we went through with. Only, I didn't retaliate against them. I just ran away. That's why I didn't go to school. They did our whole family that way."

Beside his bed each night there stands three objects that represent much of his life – a guitar, a Bible, and a shotgun.

"I can't play guitar any more, but I can touch the strings," he said.

For all the harsh things he has suffered at the hands of others, Jones insists his resolve in helping the less fortunate in life will never be stopped as long as he is able to do something for someone.

"We will never give it up," he said. "I just hope somewhere along the way that people can remember what we have done and that they will do something, too."

Linda Hudson Hoagland

Made in the USA
Columbia, SC
02 February 2022